COAL

COAL

Audre Lorde

W · W · NORTON & COMPANY · INC ·

NEW YORK

Some of the poems in this book appeared earlier in two books by the author: *The First Cities,* published by the Poets Press, New York, in 1968, copyright 1968 by Audre Lorde; and *Cables to Rage,* Volume Nine in the Heritage series published by Paul Breman, London, in 1970, © Audre Geraldin Lord 1970.

Library of Congress Cataloging in Publication Data
Lorde, Audre.
  Coal.
  Poems.
  I. Title.
  PS3562.075C6   811'.5'4   76–4971
ISBN 0–393–04439–4
ISBN 0–393–04446–7 pbk.

First Edition

1 2 3 4 5 6 7 8 9 0

To the People of Sun,
That We May All Better Understand

"If we run fast enough
the winds will not catch us."

Beth Rollins

Contents

I

Rites of Passage   3
Father Son and Holy Ghost   4
Coal   6
Rooming Houses Are Old Women   7
The Woman Thing   9
Oaxaca   10
Summer Oracle   11
Generation   13
A Family Resemblance   14
Song   15

II

On a Night Of the Full Moon   19
Now That I Am Forever with Child   21
What My Child Learns of the Sea   22
Spring People   23
Poem for a Poet   24
Story Books on a Kitchen Table   27
Pirouette   28
Hard Love Rock   29
Father the Year Has Fallen   30
Gemini   31
Bridge through My Windows   32
Conversations in Crisis   33
The Maiden   34

III

When the Saints Come Marching in   37
On Midsummer's Eve   38

Dreams Bite   39
Suspension   41
A Child Shall Lead   42
Afterlove   43
The Dozens   45
And What about the Children   46
For the King and Queen of Summer   47
Fantasy and Conversation   48
Paperweight   49

         IV

Martha   53

         V

Memorial I   65
Memorial II   66
The Songless Lark   67
Anniversary   68
Second Spring   69
To a Girl Who Knew What Side Her Bread Was
     Buttered on   70

I

Rites of Passage

Now rock the boat to a fare-thee-well.
Once we suffered dreaming
into the place where the children are playing
their child's games
where the children are hoping
knowledge survives if
unknowing
they follow the game
without winning.

Their fathers are dying
back to the freedom of wise children
playing at knowing
their fathers are dying
whose deaths will not free them
of growing from knowledge
of knowing
when the game becomes foolish
a dangerous pleading
for time out of power.

Quick
children kiss us
we are growing
through dream.

Father Son and Holy Ghost

I have not ever seen my father's grave.

Not that his judgement eyes have been
forgotten
nor his great hands' print
on our evening doorknobs
   one half turn each night
   and he would come
   drabbled with the world's business
   massive and silent as the whole day's wish
   ready to redefine each of our shapes—
but that now the evening doorknobs wait
and do not recognize us as we pass.

Each week a different woman—
regular as his one quick glass each evening—
pulls up the grass his stillness grows
calling it weed. Each week
A different woman has my mother's face
and he, who time has,
changeless,
must be amazed
who knew and loved but one.

My father died in silence, loving creation
and well-defined response.
He lived

still judgements on familiar things
and died
knowing a January 15th that year me.

Lest I go into dust
I have not ever seen my father's grave.

Coal

I
is the total black, being spoken
from the earth's inside.
There are many kinds of open
how a diamond comes into a knot of flame
how sound comes into a word, coloured
by who pays what for speaking.

Some words are open like a diamond
on glass windows
singing out within the passing crash of sun
Then there are words like stapled wagers
in a perforated book,—buy and sign and tear apart—
and come whatever wills all chances
the stub remains
an ill-pulled tooth with a ragged edge.
Some words live in my throat
breeding like adders. Others know sun
seeking like gypsies over my tongue
to explode through my lips
like young sparrows bursting from shell.
Some words
bedevil me.

Love is a word, another kind of open.
As the diamond comes into a knot of flame
I am Black because I come from the earth's inside
now take my word for jewel in the open light.

Rooming Houses Are Old Women

Rooming houses are old women
rocking dark windows into their whens
waiting incomplete circles
rocking
rent office to stoop to
community bathrooms to gas rings and
under-bed boxes of once useful garbage
city issued with a twice monthly check
and the young men next door
with their loud midnight parties
and fishy rings left in the bathtub
no longer arouse them
from midnight to mealtime no stops inbetween
light breaking to pass through jumbled up windows
and who was it who married the widow that Buzzie's son
   messed with?

To Welfare and insult from the slow shuffle
from dayswork to shopping bags
heavy with leftovers

Rooming houses
are old women waiting
searching
through darkening windows
the end or beginning of agony
old women seen through half-ajar doors
hoping
they are not waiting

but being
the entrance to somewhere
unknown and desired
but not new.

The Woman Thing

The hunters are back from beating the winter's face
in search of a challenge or task
in search of food
making fresh tracks for their children's hunger
they do not watch the sun
they cannot wear its heat for a sign
of triumph or freedom;
The hunters are treading heavily homeward
through snow that is marked
with their own bloody footprints.
emptyhanded, the hunters return
snow-maddened, sustained by their rages.

In the night after food they may seek
young girls for their amusement. But now
the hunters are coming
and the unbaked girls flee from their angers.
All this day I have craved
food for my child's hunger
Emptyhanded the hunters come shouting
injustices drip from their mouths
like stale snow melted in sunlight.

Meanwhile
the woman thing my mother taught me
bakes off its covering of snow
like a rising blackening sun.

Oaxaca

Beneath the carving drag of wood
the land moves slowly.
But lightning comes.

Growing their secret in brown earth
spread like a woman
daring
is weary work for still-eyed men
who break the earth
nursing their seed
and a hard watch through the dry season.
Yet at the edge of bright thin day
past the split plow—they look
to the hills—to the brewing thunder
for the storm is known.

The land moves slowly.
Though the thunder's eve
can crack with a flash
the glass-brittle crust of a mountains face
the land moves slowly.
All a man's strength in his son's arms
to carve one sleeve
into rock defiant earth
and the spread land waits.

Slow long the plowing
through dry-season brown
and the land moves slowly.

But lightning comes.

Summer Oracle

Without expectation
there is no end
to the shocks of morning
or even a small summer.

Now the image is fire
blackening the vague lines
into defiance across the city.
the image is fire
sun warming us in a cold country
barren of symbols for love.

But I have forsaken order
and imagine you into fire
untouchable in a magician's cloak
covered with signs of destruction and birth
sewn with griffins and arrows and hammers
and gold sixes stitched into your hem.
your fingers draw fire
but still the old warlocks shun you
for no gourds ring in your sack
no spells bring forth peace
and I am still fruitless and hungry
this summer
the peaches are flinty and juiceless
and cry sour worms.

The image is fire
flaming over you burning off excess
like the blaze planters start

to burn off bagasse from the canefields
after a harvest.

The image is fire
the high sign that rules our summer
I smell it in the charred breezes blowing over
your body
close
hard
essential
under its cloak of lies.

Generation

How the young attempt and are broken
differs from age to age
We were brown free girls
love singing beneath our skin
sun in our hair in our eyes
sun our fortune
and the wind had made us golden
made us gay.

In a season of limited power
we wept out our promises
And these are the children we try now
for temptations that wear our face.
But who comes back from our latched cities of falsehood
to warn them that the road to nowhere
is slippery with our blood
to warn them
they need not drink the river to get home
since we have purchased bridges
with our mothers' bloody gold;—
for now we are more than kin
who come to share
not only blood
but the bloodiness of our failures.

How the young are tempted and betrayed
into slaughter or conformity
is a turn of the mirror
time's question only.

A Family Resemblance

My sister has my hair my mouth my eyes
and I presume her trustless.
When she was young and open to any fever
wearing gold like a veil of fortune on her face
she waited through each rain a dream of light.
But the sun came up
burning our eyes like crystal
bleaching the sky of promise and
my sister stood
Black, unblessed and unbelieving
shivering in the first cold show of love.

I saw her gold become an arch
where nightmare hunted
down the porches of restless night.
Now through echoes of denial
she walks a bleached side of reason.
Secret now
my sister never waits
nor mourns the gold that wandered from her bed.

My sister has my tongue
and all my flesh
unanswered
and I presume her trustless
as a stone.

Song

The wild trees have bought me
and will sell you a wind
in the forest of falsehoods
where your search must not end

for their roots are not wise.
Strip our loving of dream
pay its secrets to thunder
and ransom me home.

Beware oaks in laughter
know hemlock is lying
when she sings of defiance.
The sand words she is saying

will sift over and bury
while the pale moons I hate
seduce you in phases
through oceans of light.

And the wild trees shall sell me
for their safety from lightning
to sand that will flay me
for the next evening's planting.

They will fill my limp skin
with wild dreams from their root
and grow from my flesh
new handfuls of hate

till our ransom is wasted
and the morning speaks out
in a thin voice of wisdom
that loves me too late.

II

On a Night of the Full Moon

Out of my flesh that hungers
and my mouth that knows
comes the shape I am seeking
for reason.
The curve of your waiting body
fits my waiting hand
your breasts warm as sunlight
your lips quick as young birds
between your thighs the sweet
sharp taste of limes.

Thus I hold you
frank in my heart's eye
in my skin's knowing
as my fingers conceive your flesh
I feel your stomach
moving against me.

Before the moon wanes again
we shall come together.

And I would be the moon
spoken over your beckoning flesh
breaking against reservations
beaching thought
my hands at your high tide
over and under inside you
and the passing of hungers

attended, forgotten.

Darkly risen
the moon speaks
my eyes
judging your roundness
delightful.

Now That I Am Forever
with Child

How the days went
while you were blooming within me
I remember each upon each—
the swelling changed planes of my body
and how you first fluttered, then jumped
and I thought it was my heart.

How the days wound down
and the turning of winter
I recall, with you growing heavy
against the wind. I thought
now her hands
are formed, and her hair
has started to curl
now her teeth are done
now she sneezes.
Then the seed opened
I bore you one morning just before spring
My head rang like a fiery piston
my legs were towers between which
A new world was passing.

Since then
I can only distinguish
one thread within running hours
You, flowing through selves
toward You.

What My Child Learns of the Sea

What my child learns of the sea
of the summer thunders
of the riddles that hide in the curve of spring
she will learn in my twilights
and childlike
revise every autumn.

What my child learns
as her winters grow into time
has ripened in my own body
to enter her eyes with first light.

This is why
more than blood
or the milk I have given
one day a strange girl will step
to the back of a mirror
cutting my ropes
of sea and thunder and spring.
Of the way she will taste her autumns—
toast-brittle or warmer than sleep—
and the words she will use for winter
I stand already condemned.

Spring People

for Jonno

What anger in my hard-won bones
or heritage of water
makes me reject the april
and fear to walk upon the earth
in spring?

At springtime and evening
I recall how we came
like new thunder
beating the earth
leaving the taste of rain and sunset
all our hungers before us.
Away from the peace of half truths
and springtime passing unsaid
we came in the touch of fire
came to the sun
lay with a wild earth
until spent and knowing
we brought forth our young.

Now insolent aprils bedevil us—
earthy conceits—
to remind us that all else is forfeit
only our blood-hungry children
remember
what face we had
what startling eyes.

Poem for a Poet

I think of a coffin's quiet
when I sit in the world of my car
separate and observing
with the windows closed and washed clean
by the rain. I like to sit there
watching the other worlds pass. Yesterday evening
I sat in my car on Sheridan Square
flat and broke and a little bit damp
thinking about money and rain and how
the Village broads with their narrow hips
rolled like drunken shovels
down Christopher Street.

Then I saw you unmistakeably
darting out from between a police car and
what used to be Atkin's all-night diner—
where we sat making bets the last time I saw you
on how many busts we could count through the plateglass
    window
in those last skinny hours before dawn
with our light worded-out but still burning
and the earlier evening's promise dregs in our coffee cups—
and I saw you dash out and turn left at the corner
your beard spiky with rain and refusing
shelter under your chin.

But I had thought you were dead Jarrell
struck down by a car at sunset on a North Carolina road
or were you the driver
tricked into a fatal swerve by some twilit shadow

or was that Frank O'Hara
or Conrad Kent Rivers
and you
the lonely spook in a Windy City motel
draped in the secrets of your convulsive death
all alone
all poets all loved and dying alone
that final death
less real than those deaths you lived
and for which I forgave you?

I watched you hurry down Fourth Street Jarrell
from the world of my car in the rain
remembering that Spring Festival Night
at Womens College in North Carolina
and wasn't that world a coffin's retreat
of spring whispers romance and rhetoric
Untouched
by the wind buffeting up the road from Greensboro
and nobody mentioned the Black Revolution
or Sit-Ins or Freedom Rides or SNCC
or cattle-prods in Jackson Mississippi—
where I was to find myself how many years later:

You were mistaken that night and I told you
later in a letter beginning—Dear Jarrell
if you sit in one place long enough
the whole world will pass you by . . .
you were wrong when you said I took
living too seriously
meaning you were afraid I might take you
too seriously
you shouldn't have worried because
although I dug you too much
to put you down

I never took you at all
except as a good piece of my first journey south
except as I take you now
gladly and separate at a distance
and wondering
as I have so often
how come being so cool
you weren't also a little bit
black.

And also why you have returned
to this dying city
and what piece of me is it then
buried down there in North Carolina.

Story Books on a Kitchen Table

Out of her womb of pain my mother spat me
into her ill-fitting harness of despair
into her deceits
where anger re-conceived me
piercing my eyes like arrows
pointed by her nightmare
of who I was not
becoming.

Going away
she left in her place
iron maidens to protect me
and for my food
the wrinkled milk of legend
where I wandered through the lonely rooms of afternoon
wrapped in nightmares
from the Orange and Red and Yellow
Purple and Blue and Green
Fairy Books
where white witches ruled
over the empty kitchen table
and never wept
or offered gold
nor any kind enchantment
for the vanished mother
of a black girl.

Pirouette

I saw
your hands on my lips like blind needles
blunted
from sewing up stone
and
    where are you from
                you said
your hands reading over my lips for
some road through uncertain night
for your feet to examine home
where are you from
                you said
your hands
on my lips like thunder
promising rain

a land where all lovers are mute.

And
    why are you weeping
                you said
your hands in my doorway like rainbows
following rain
why are you weeping?

I am come home.

Hard Love Rock

Today I heard my heart screeching like a subway train
loudly enough to remind me it was still human
loudly enough to hurt
but telling me still
you were a ghost I had
better left in the cradle,
telling me still
that our tracks ran around
instead of straight out past the sewers
that I would have nothing for barter left
not even the print of love's grain
pressed into my flesh from our wooden cross
left splintered and shapeless
after the slaughter.

And when it was over
only pain.

Father the Year Has Fallen

Father the year has fallen.
Leaves bedeck my careful flesh like stone.
One shard of brilliant summer pierced me
and remains.
By this only
unregenerate bone
I am not dead, but waiting.
When the last warmth is gone
I shall bear in the snow.

Gemini

Moon minded the sun goes farther from us
split into swirled days, smoked,
unhungered, and unkempt
no longer young.

All the earth falls down
like lost light frightened out between my fingers.
Here at the end of night
our love is a burnt out ocean
a dry worded, brittle bed.
Our roots, once nourished by the cool lost water
cry out—"Remind us!"—and the oyster world
cries out its pearls like tears.

And was this the wild calling I heard in the long night past
wrapped in a stone closed house?
I wakened to moon and the sound breached dark
and thinking a new word spoken—
some promise made—
broke through the screaming night
seeking a gateway out

But the night was dark
and love was a burning fence about my house.

Bridge through My Window

In curve scooped out and necklaced with light
burst pearls stream down my out-stretched arms to earth.
Oh bridge my sister bless me before I sleep
the wild air is lengthening
and I am tried beyond strength or bearing
over water.

Love, we are both shorelines
a left country
where time suffices
and the right land
where pearls roll into earth and spring up day.
joined, our bodies have passage into one
without merging
as this slim necklace is anchored into night.

And while the we conspires
to make secret its two eyes
we search the other shore
for some crossing home.

Conversations in Crisis

I speak to you as a friend speaks
or a true lover
not out of friendship nor love
but for a clear meeting
of self upon self
in sight of our hearth
but without fire.

I cherish your words that ring
like late summer thunders
to sing without octave
and fade, having spoken the season.
But I hear the false heat of this voice
as it dries up the sides of your words
coaxing melodies from your tongue
and this curled music is treason.

Must I die in your fever—
or, as the flames wax, take cover
in your heart's culverts
crouched like a stranger
under the scorched leaves of your other burnt loves
until the storm passes over?

The Maiden

Once I was immortal beside an ocean
having the names of night
and the first men came
with sledges of fire
driving the sun.

I was brought forth in the moonpit of a virgin
condemned to light
to a dry world's endless mornings
sweeping the moon away
and wherever I fled
seeking a new road home
morning had harrowed the endless rivers
to nest in the dried out bed
of my mother sea.

Time drove the moon down to crescent
and they found me
mortal
beside a moon's crater
mouthing the ocean names of night.

III

When the Saints Come Marching in

Plentiful sacrifice and believers in redemption
are all that is needed
so any day now
I expect some new religion
to rise up like tear gas
from the streets of New York
erupting like the rank pavement smell
released by the garbage-trucks'
baptismal drizzle.

The high priests have been ready and waiting
with their incense pans full of fire.
I do not know the rituals
the exhaltations
nor what name of the god
the survivors will worship
I only know she will be terrible
and very busy
and very old.

On Midsummer's Eve

Ride the swing season
hawk gander or stallion
evading the light
you survive
lost
among the stiff trees
laying rebellious eggs
that roll and splatter
in your enemy sun.

your arrows rot
in a muddy quiver
while the quick vowels
flutter and plummet
through stiff trees without echo
you do not fly.
you do not fly.

Your words explode
under silence
returning
to rot
in the changing season
I ride with the sun
passing
returning again
and again
you do not learn
you do not learn.

Dreams Bite

I

Dreams bite.
The dreamer and his legends
arm at the edge of purpose.

Waking
I see the people of winter
put off their masks
to stain the earth red with blood
while
on the outer edges of sleep
the people of sun
are carving
their own children
into monuments
of war.

II

When I am absolute
at once
with the black earth
fire
I make
my nows
and power is spoken
peace
at rest and
hungry means never

or alone
I shall love
again

When I am obsolete.

Suspension

We entered silence
before the clock struck.

Red wine into crystal
is not quite
fallen
air solidifies around your mouth
once-wind has sucked the curtains in
like fright against the evening wall
prepared for storm   before the room
exhales   your lips
unfold.
Within their sudden opening
I hear
the clock begin
to speak again.

I remember now with the filled crystal
shattered, the wind-whipped curtains
bound and the cold storm
finally broken
how the room felt
when
your word was spoken—

Warm
as the center of your palm
and as unfree.

A Child Shall Lead

I have a child
whose feet are blind
on every road
but silence.

My boy has
lovely foolish lips
but cannot find
his way to sun

And I am grown
past knowledge.

Afterlove

In what had been a pathway
inbetween
our bed and a shared bathroom
broken hours lap at my heels
reaching my toothbrush
finally
I see
wide valleys filled with water
folding into myself
alone
I cross them into the shower
the tiles right themselves
in retreat
my skin thrills
bruised and battered
as thunderspray splatters
plasma on my horizons
when no more rain comes
I cast me out lightly
returning
on tiptoe
shifting and lurching
against my eyes
plastic curtains
I hung
last December
watching the sun flee
through patterns
spinning
always and never

returning
I spiced my armpits
courting the solstice
and never once did I abandon
believing
I would contrive
to make my world
whole again.

The Dozens

Nothing says that you must see me in the street
with us so close together at that red light
that a blind man could have smelled his grocer—
and nothing says that you must
say hello
as we pass in the street,
but we have known each other too well
in the dark
for this,
and it hurts me when you do not speak.

And no one you were with was quite so fine
that I won't remember this and
suffer you in turn and
in my own fashion which is certainly
not in the street.
For I can count on my telephone
ringing some evening and you
exploding into my room through the receiver
kissing and licking my ear. . . .

I hope you will learn your thing
at least
from some of those spiteful noseless
people who surround you
before the centipede in you
runs out of worlds
one for each foot.

And What About the Children

Now we've made a child.
and the dire predictions
have changed into wild
grim
speculations;
still the negatives
are waiting
watching
and the relatives
keep right on
Touching . . .
    and how much curl
    is right for a girl?
But if it is said
at some future date
that my son's head
is on straight
he won't care
about his
hair
nor give a damn
whose wife
I am.

For the King and
Queen of Summer

The land of flowers is dusty
and covered with jewels.
Alan writes that Ceylon
is heavy with topaz and rubies
and the stink of rotting lotus.

He will return
with opals and moonstones
around his neck
and a crippled monkey named Buddha
in his back pocket.

When he comes home
the Red Queen
will cook rice-cream and pray
for a second coming
as she fiercely shields the children
until their bones grow stronger.

She teaches them royal forebearance
while the crippled monkey
quite at home
picks his nose
as he makes a shithouse
under their throne.

Fantasy and Conversation

Speckled frogs leap from my mouth
to drown in the coffee
between our wisdoms
and decision.

I could smile
and turn these frogs to pearls
speak of love, our making
our giving.
And if the spell works
shall I break down
or build what is broken
into a new house
shook with confusion

Shall I strike
before our magic
turns colour?

Paperweight

Paper is neither kind nor cruel
merely white in its neutrality
I have for reality now
the brown bar of my arm
moving in broken rhythm
across this dead place.

All the poems I have ever written
are historical reviews of some now-absorbed country
a small judgement
hawking and coughing them up
I have ejected them not unlike children.
Now my throat is clear
and perhaps I shall speak again.

All the poems I have ever written
make a small book shaped like another me
called by yesterday's names
the shedding of a past in patched conceits
moulted like snake skin—
a book of leavings.
I can do anything with them I wish
I can love them or hate them
use them for comfort or warmth
tissues or decoration
dolls or japanese baskets
blankets or spells.
I can use them for magic
lanterns or music
advice or small council

for napkins or past-times or
disposable diapers
I can make fire from them
or kindling
songs or paper chains

Or fold them all into a paper fan
with which to cool my husband's dinner.

IV

Martha

I

Martha this is a catalog of days
passing before you looked again.
Someday you will browse and order them
at will, or in your necessities.

I have taken a house at the Jersey shore
this summer. It is not my house.
Today the lightning bugs came.

On the first day you were dead.
With each breath the skin of your face moved
falling in like crumpled muslin.
We scraped together the smashed image of flesh
preparing a memory. No words.
No words.

On the eighth day
you startled the doctors
speaking from your deathplace
to reassure us that you were trying.

Martha these are replacement days
should you ever need them
given for those you once demanded and never found.
May this trip be rewarding;
no one can fault you again Martha
for answering necessity too well
and the gods who honor hard work
will keep this second coming
free from that lack of choice

which hindered your first journey
to this Tarot house.

They said
no hope no dreaming
accept this case of flesh as evidence
of life without fire
and wrapped you in an electric blanket
kept ten degrees below life.
Fetal hands curled inward on the icy sheets
your bed was so cold
the bruises could not appear.

On the second day I knew you were alive
because the grey flesh of your face
suffered.

I love you and cannot feel you less than Martha
I love you and cannot split this shaved head
from Martha's pushy straightness
asking
in a smash of mixed symbols
How long must I wander here
in this final house of my father?

On the Solstice I was in Providence.
You know this town because you visited friends here.
It rained in Providence on the Solstice—
I remember we passed through here twice
on route Six through Providence to the Cape
where we spent our second summer
trying for peace or equity, even.
It always seemed to be raining
by the time we got to Providence.
The Kirschenbaums live in Providence

and Blossom and Barry
and Frances. And Frances.
Martha I am in love again.
Listen, Frances, I said on the Solstice
our summer has started.
Today we are witches and with enough energy
to move mountains back.
Think of Martha.

Back in my hideous city
I saw you today. Your hair has grown
and your armpits are scented
by some careful attendant.
Your *Testing testing testing*
explosive syllables warning me
Of *The mountain has fallen into dung*—
no Martha remember remember Martha—
Warning
Dead flowers will not come to your bed again.
The sun has started south
our season is over.

Today you opened your eyes, giving
a blue-filmed history to your mangled words.
They help me understand
how you are teaching yourself to learn
again.

I need you need me
Je suis Martha I do not speak french kissing
Oh Wow. Black and . . . Black and . . . beautiful?
Black and becoming
somebody else maybe Erica maybe who sat
in the fourth row behind us in high school
but I never took French with you Martha

and who is this *Madame Erudite*
who is not me?

I find you today in a womb full of patients
blue-robed in various convalescences.
Your eyes are closed you are propped
into a wheelchair, cornered,
in a parody of resting.
The bright glue of tragedy plasters all eyes
to a television set in the opposite corner
where a man is dying
step by step
in the american ritual going.
Someone has covered you
for this first public appearance
in a hospital gown, a badge of your next step.
Evocative voices flow from the set
and the horror is thick
in this room full of broken and mending receptions.

But no one has told you what it's all about Martha
someone has shot another Kennedy
we are drifting closer to what you predicted
and your darkness is indeed speaking
Robert Kennedy is dying Martha
but not you not you not you
he has a bullet in his brain Martha
surgery was never considered for you
since there was no place to start
and no one intended to run you down on a highway
being driven home at 7:30 on a low summer evening
I gave a reading in Harlem that night
and who shall we try for this shaven head now
in the courts of heart Martha
where his murder is televised over and over
with residuals

they have caught the man who shot Robert Kennedy
who was another one of difficult journeys—
he has a bullet in his brain Martha
and much less of a chance than you.

On the first day of July you warned me again
the threads are broken
you darkened into explosive angers and
refused to open your eyes, humming interference
your thoughts are not over Martha
they are you and their task is
to remember Martha
we can help with the other
the mechanics of blood and bone
and you cut through the pain of my words
to warn me again
testing testing whoever passes
must tear out their hearing aids
for the duration.
I hear you explaining Neal
my husband whoever must give me a present
he has to give me
himself where I can find him for
where can he look at himself
in the mirror I am making
or over my bed where the window
is locked into battle with a wall?

Now I sit in New Jersey with lightning bugs and mosquitoes
typing and thinking of you.
Tonight you started seizures
which they say is a temporary relapse
but this lake is far away Martha
and I sit unquiet in New Jersey
thinking of you
I Ching the Book of Changes

says I am impertinent to ask of you obliquely
but I have no direct question
only need.
When I cast an oracle today
it spoke of the Abyssmal again
which of all the Hexagrams
is very difficult but very promising
in it water finds its own level, flowing
out from the lowest point.
And I cast another also that cautioned
the superior man to seek his strength
only in its own season.
Martha what did we learn from our brief season
when the summer grackles rang in my walls?
one and one is too late now
you journey through darkness alone
leafless I sit far from my present house
and the grackles' voices are dying
we shall love each other here if ever at all.

II

Yes foolish prejudice lies
I hear you Martha
that you would never harm my children
but you have forgotten their names
and that you are Elizabeth's godmother.
And you offer me coral rings, watches
even your body
if I will help you sneak home.

No Martha my blood is not muddy my hands
are not dirty to touch
Martha I do not know your night nurse's name
even though she is black

yes I did live in Brighton Beach once
which is almost Rockaway
one bitter winter
but not with your night nurse Martha
and yes I agree this is one hell
of a summer.

No you cannot walk yet Martha
and no the medicines you are given
to quiet your horrors
have not affected your brain
yes it is very hard to think but
it is getting easier and yes Martha
we have loved each other and yes I hope
we still can
no Martha I do not know if we shall ever
sleep in each other's arms again.

III

It is the middle of August and you are alive
to discomfort. You have been moved
into a utility room across the hall
from the critical ward because your screaming
disturbs the other patients
your bedside table has been moved also
which means you will be there for a while
a favorite now with the floor nurses
who put up a sign on the utility room door
I'M MARTHA HERE DO NOT FORGET ME
PLEASE KNOCK.

A golden attendant named Sukie
bathes you as you proposition her
she is very pretty and very gentle.

The frontal lobe of the brain governs inhibitions
the damage is after all slight
and they say the screaming will pass.

Your daughter Dorrie promises you
will be as good as new, Mama
who only wants to be *Bad as the old.*

I want some truth good hard truth
a sign of youth
we were all young once we had
a good thing going
now I'm making a plan
for a dead rabbit a rare rabbit.
I am dying goddammit dying am I
Dying?
Death is a word you can say now
pain is mortal
I am dying for god's sake won't someone please
get me a doctor PLEASE
your screams beat against our faces as you yell
begging relief from the blank cruelty
of a thousand nurses.
A moment of silence breaks
as you accumulate fresh sorrows
then through your pain-fired face
you slip me a wink

Martha Winked.

IV

Your face straightens into impatience
with the loads of shit you are handed

'You're doing just fine Martha what time is it Martha'
'What did you have for supper tonight Martha'
testing testing whoever passes for Martha
you weary of it.

All the people you must straighten out
pass your bedside in the utility room
bringing you cookies
and hoping
you will be kinder than they were.

Go away Mama and Bubie
for 30 years you made me believe
I was shit you shat out for the asking
but I'm not and you'd better believe it
right now would you kindly
stop rubbing my legs
and GET THE HELL OUT OF HERE.
Next week Bubie bring Teglach
your old favorite
and will you be kinder Martha
then we were to the shell the cocoon
out of which the you is emerging?

V

No one you were can come so close
to death without dying
into another Martha.
I await you
as we all await her
fearing her honesty
fearing
we may neither love nor dismiss

Martha with the dross burned away
fearing
condemnation from the essential.

You cannot get closer to death than this Martha
the nearest you've come to living yourself.

Memorial I

If you come as softly
as wind within the trees
you may hear what I hear
see what sorrow sees.

If you come as lightly
as the threading dew
I shall take you gladly
nor ask more of you.

You may sit beside me
silent as a breath
and only those who stay dead
shall remember death.

If you come I will be silent
nor speak harsh words to you—
I will not ask you why, now,
nor how, nor what you knew.

But we shall sit here softly
beneath two different years
and the rich earth between us
shall drink our tears.

Memorial II

Genevieve
what are you seeing
in my mirror this morning
peering out from behind my eyes
like a hungry bird
Are you seeking the shape of a girl
I have grown less and less
to resemble
or do you remember
I could not accept your face dying
I do not know you now
But surely your vision stayed
stronger than mine
Genevieve tell me
where do the dead girls wander
after their summer?

I wish I could see you again
far from me even
birdlike
flying into the sun
your eyes
blind me Genevieve.

The Songless Lark

Sun shines so brightly on the hill
that I can see each day
patches of snow that fell this spring
before you went away.

And now that summer's near at hand
below the meadow springs
behind the trees at dawnlight
a songless lark now sings.

Anniversary

The bitter tears are stone
but one quick breath
remembers love
and the long years you've lain
bride to the thunder
sister to fallen rain
who ate a bitter fruit
to dance with death.

We have no right to love
now you are dead
who could not hold you here.
Our tears
water an alien grass.
All has been said
and you have walked in silence
many years.

But April came today.
though spring comes ever
even in the empty years
since you have slept
it was in April
that you chose to sever
young love and self
and I remembered
and I wept.

Second Spring

We have no passions left to love the spring
who have suffered autumn as we did, alone
walking through dominions of a browning laughter
carrying our loneliness, our loving and our pain.

How shall we know another spring
For there will come no flower where was fruit before
and we have little use for spring's relentless seeking
who walked the long, unquestioned path
straight into autumn's trailing arms
who saw the summer passions wither
into dry leaves to hide our naked tears.

Autumn teaches bearing
and new sun will warm our proud and cautious feet
but spring came once
and we have seen the road that led through summer
beautiful and bright as clover on a hill
become a vast appalling wilderness and rain
while we stood still
racked on the autumn's weeping
binding cold love to us
with the corners of her shroud.

To a Girl Who Knew What Side Her Bread Was Buttered On

He, through the eyes of the first marauder
saw her, his catch of bright thunder, heaping
tea and bread for her guardian dead
crunching the nut-dry words they said
and, thinking the bones were sleeping.
he broke through the muffled afternoon
calling an end to their ritual's tune
with lightning-like disorder:

'Leave these bones, Love! Come away
from their summer breads with the flavour of hay—
your guards can watch the shards of our catch
warming *our* bones on some winter's day!'

Like an ocean of straws the old bones rose up
Fearing his threat of a second death;
and he had little time to wonder
at the silence of bright thunder
as, with a smile of pity and stealth,
she buttered fresh scones for her guardian bones
and they trampled him into the earth.